MONARCH BUTTERFLIES

MONARCH BUTTERFLIES

CHARLES ROTTER

THE CHILD'S WORLD

PHOTO RESEARCH

Charles Rotter/Gary Lopez Productions

PHOTO CREDITS

COMSTOCK/Townsend Dickinson:
front cover, 6, 14
COMSTOCK/George Lepp: back cover,
2, 10, 13, 17, 18, 21, 23, 27, 28, 31
Jeff Foott: 9, 24

This book is a presentation of Newfield Publications, Inc.
For information about Newfield Publications book clubs for children
write to: **Newfield Publications, Inc.,**
4343 Equity Drive, Columbus, Ohio 43228.

Published by arrangement with The Child's World, Inc.
Newfield Publications is a federally registered
trademark of Newfield Publications, Inc.

1996 edition

Library of Congress Cataloging-in-Publication Data
Rotter, Charles.
Monarch butterflies / Charles Murray Rotter.
p. cm.
Summary: Introduces the physical characteristics,
habits, and life cycle of the monarch butterfly.
ISBN 0-89565-840-2
1. Monarch butterfly--Juvenile literature.
[1. Monarch butterfly.   2. Butterflies.]   I. Title.
QL561.D3R68   1993   92-4913
595.78'9--dc20   CIP
                                                  AC

To Melissa, who was always there when I needed her.

Have you ever seen a monarch butterfly? They live all over North America. Monarch butterflies live in Canada, in Mexico, and in the United States. You can see them flying through the air or resting on trees and flowers. Sometimes, if you are quiet and move very slowly, you can get a close look.

Monarch butterflies can fly very far. In the fall, they fly all the way from Canada to Mexico. That's over 2,000 miles! In the spring and summer, they make the return trip to Canada.

Monarch butterflies can fly only when they are fully grown. Monarch butterflies don't have the same shape all their lives. When they are young, monarchs look more like small worms than butterflies. A monarch with this shape is called a *caterpillar*. All butterflies begin their lives as caterpillars. Young caterpillars look for food as soon as they hatch from their tiny eggs. Baby caterpillars must take care of themselves. Their mothers and fathers do not help them at all.

Monarch caterpillars eat only one kind of food—a plant called *milkweed*. Most animals don't eat milkweed because it tastes bad and can make them sick. Monarch caterpillars don't mind the taste. They eat as much milkweed as they can. They even store some of the milkweed in their bodies. This makes them taste bad to other animals. The monarch's bright colors are its way of saying, "I'm a monarch. Don't eat me or I'll make you sick."

Monarch caterpillars spend most of their time eating, so they grow very fast. After only three weeks, they weigh thousands of times more than they did when they were born. Monarch caterpillars try to get as big and fat as they can. They are storing away food for the next part of their life.

Once a caterpillar is fat enough, it looks for a place to change into its next shape. While in this next shape, the monarch can't move. To be safe, the caterpillar looks for a place away from blowing grass and leaves. The spot also must be hard for other animals to see. When the caterpillar finds an out-of-the-way place, it hangs upside down and firmly attaches itself. The caterpillar then changes into a shorter and rounder shape called a *pupa*.

The pupa has soft skin when it first forms. After about a day, the skin hardens into a jewel-like shell called a *chrysalis*. The monarch lives within the chrysalis for about two weeks. During this time, the pupa doesn't eat. It lives on food that it stored away when it was a hungry caterpillar. Inside the chrysalis, the pupa changes. It grows wings and legs. Even its eyes grow bigger. This next shape is its last one. The monarch will leave the chrysalis as a full-grown butterfly.

Usually, the monarch leaves the chrysalis on a calm, sunny day. The butterfly struggles to twist out of the chrysalis. It uses its new legs to hold onto the branch or twig. This is a dangerous time for the butterfly. The monarch must let its wings dry out and harden before it can fly. If it is windy, the monarch could be blown away and injured.

Like the caterpillar, the monarch butterfly is brightly colored. It still carries some milkweed in its body. The bright colors warn other animals to stay away, just as the bright colors of the caterpillar do.

In a very short time, the butterfly begins to fly. At first it flies from flower to flower in search of food. When the monarch was a caterpillar, its mouth was shaped for eating milkweed. As a butterfly, the monarch lives on the sweet juice inside flowers, called *nectar*. To reach the nectar, the monarch's mouth is shaped like a long, thin tube.

Soon the butterfly begins to fly on its long trip. If the monarch is born in the fall, it heads south toward Mexico. Along the way, the butterfly joins up with many other monarchs. The butterflies fly during the day and rest at night. Sometimes hundreds of monarchs gather at the same resting spot.

The monarchs fly south to get away from the cold winter in the North. They spend the winter in the southern parts of North America where it's warm. This could be in Mexico or the lower part of the United States. Some of the female monarchs lay eggs, which develop into new butterflies. The monarchs live in the South until spring arrives. Then they start to fly north.

On the return trip north, many of the female monarchs lay eggs on milkweed plants. The caterpillars that hatch from the eggs develop into new butterflies. Once they can fly, the young monarchs join in the journey north. The older butterflies don't live long enough to make it all the way back home. But new monarchs keep hatching and heading north.

The butterflies that make it all the way north may be the great-great-grandchildren of the ones that flew south in the fall. Many other animals move with the changing seasons. However, the monarch butterfly is one of the few whose children finish the round-trip.